D1518669

Wedges

by Joanne Mattern

BELLWETHER MEDIA • MINNEAPOLIS, MN

Note to Librarians, Teachers, and Parents:

Blastoff! Readers are carefully developed by literacy experts and combine standards-based content with developmentally appropriate text.

Level 1 provides the most support through repetition of high-frequency words, light text, predictable sentence patterns, and strong visual support.

Level 2 offers early readers a bit more challenge through varied simple sentences, increased text load, and less repetition of high-frequency words.

Level 3 advances early-fluent readers toward fluency through increased text and concept load, less reliance on visuals, longer sentences, and more literary language.

Level 4 builds reading stamina by providing more text per page, increased use of punctuation, greater variation in sentence patterns, and increasingly challenging vocabulary.

Level 5 encourages children to move from "learning to read" to "reading to learn" by providing even more text, varied writing styles, and less familiar topics.

Whichever book is right for your reader, Blastoff! Readers are the perfect books to build confidence and encourage a love of reading that will last a lifetime!

This edition first published in 2020 by Bellwether Media, Inc.

No part of this publication may be reproduced in whole or in part without written permission of the publisher. For information regarding permission, write to Bellwether Media, Inc., Attention: Permissions Department, 6012 Blue Circle Drive, Minnetonka, MN 55343.

Library of Congress Cataloging-in-Publication Data

Names: Mattern, Joanne, 1963- author.
Title: Wedges / by Joanne Mattern.
Description: Minneapolis, MN : Bellwether Media, Inc., 2020. | Series: Blastoff! Readers: Simple machines fun! | Includes bibliographical references and index. | Audience: 5-8. | Audience: K to grade 3.
Identifiers: LCCN 2018056037 (print) | LCCN 2018060221 (ebook) | ISBN 9781618915351 (ebook) | ISBN 9781626179950 (hardcover : alk. paper)
Subjects: LCSH: Wedges--Juvenile literature.
Classification: LCC TJ1201.W44 (ebook) | LCC TJ1201.W44 M38 2020 (print) | DDC 621.8--dc23
LC record available at https://lccn.loc.gov/2018056037

Editor: Christina Leaf   Designer: Jeffrey Kollock

Printed in the United States of America, North Mankato, MN.

Table of Contents

What Are Wedges?

Wedges are two **inclined planes** put together. The two planes meet to make a sharp edge or point.

Wedges may be skinny, like knives, or thick, like **plows**.

snowplow

Wedges are good for pushing things apart. Your front teeth are wedges that push apart food.

Wedges can also keep things in place. Doorstops hold doors open.

How Do Wedges Work?

Wedges move **force** from one place to another.

Pushing on the large end moves the force to the thin end. The thin end now has a large force!

A wedge changes the
direction of a force.

The thin edge of the wedge moves the downward force to the side.

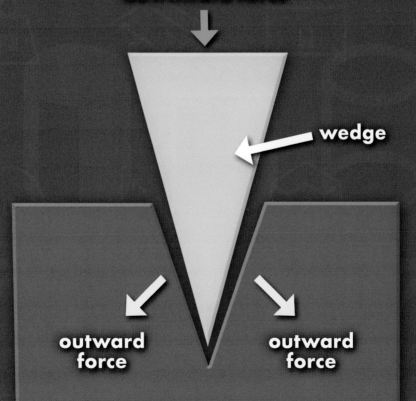

How Wedges Work

downward force

wedge

outward force

outward force

Cutting with Wedges

What You Need:

- a ball of Play-Doh
- a plastic knife

What To Do:

1. Try to split the ball of Play-Doh in half with the side of your hand. How hard is it to do?

2. Push the knife into the Play-Doh. Is it easier or harder to cut the Play-Doh in half now?

A wedge that is long and thin
can do more work with less force.
A short, wide wedge needs
more force to do the work.

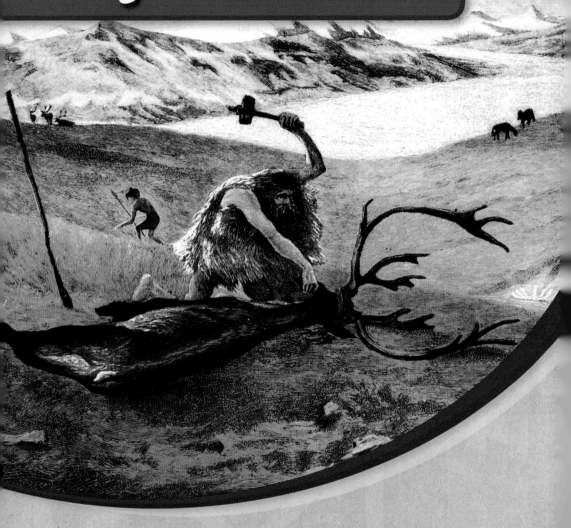

Ancient people used wedges millions of years ago.

They made axes.
These were some
of the first tools.

Today we use wedges in many ways. Axes help us chop down trees.

chisel

Chisels help us carve stones.

Wedges also hold things still.
A wedge under a short table leg
keeps the table from wobbling.
A wedge can keep a car from
rolling away!

Wedge Power!

What You Need:

- a board
- a small hammer

- a nail
- a bolt

What To Do:

1. Have an adult help you try to hammer the bolt into the board. Does it work? Why or why not?

2. Have an adult help you try to hammer a nail into the board. Does it work? Why or why not?

nose

A wedge can be part of
a **complex machine**.

Everyday Wedges

Simple

axe head

doorstop

Complex

jet plane

speedboat

The nose of a jet is a wedge.
It pushes through the air.
A wedge does a big job!

Glossary

ancient—from long ago

chisels—tools with wedges at one end that help carve, chip, or cut into something

complex machine—a machine that combines two or more simple machines

force—the amount of energy it takes to do something

inclined planes—simple machines that are flat surfaces with one end that is higher than the other

plows—machines shaped like wedges that break up soil or snow

To Learn More

AT THE LIBRARY

Dickmann, Nancy. *Wedges.* Tucson, Ariz.:
Brown Bear Books, 2018.

Rivera, Andrea. *Wedges.* Minneapolis, Minn.:
Abdo Zoom, 2017.

Weakland, Mark. *Fred Flintstone's Adventures
with Wedges: Just Split!.* North Mankato, Minn.:
Capstone Press, 2016.

ON THE WEB

FACTSURFER

Factsurfer.com gives you
a safe, fun way to find
more information.

1. Go to www.factsurfer.com.

2. Enter "wedges" into the search box
   and click 🔍.

3. Select your book cover to see a list
   of related web sites.

Index

The images in this book are reproduced through the courtesy of: Petr Salinger, front cover; Ivan Marjanovic, pp. 4-5; Tasch, p. 5; RomarioIen, p. 6; robcruse, pp. 6-7; sonsam, p. 8; AlexSava, pp. 8-9; Anrey Armyagov, pp. 10-11; Bellwether Media, pp. 12 (all), 19 (all); sima, p. 13; World History Archive/ Alamy, pp. 14-15; Sandstein/ Wikimedia Commons, p. 15; Sarita Sutthisakari, p. 16; Monkey Business Images, pp. 16-17; Oksana Volina, p. 18; sam-whitfield1, pp. 20-21; Marsan, p. 21 (axe); Paradise on Earth, p. 21 (doorstop); Fasttailwind, p. 21 (jet plane); freevideoagency, p. 21 (boat).